HIGH SAL

HIGHle
QAL

a collaboration of lyric prose

LeBeyt Seifu-Mikael

Teffera **BGZ** Teffera

lebeyt◯bqz

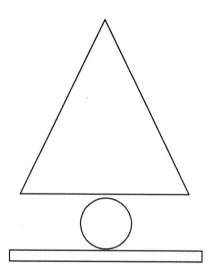

Dancehall University Books

Copyright © 2020 DHU Books Long Beach, California
ISBN# 978-1-7320875-2-1
Printed in the United States of America

Dedications

This work is dedicated to the universal-balance of creation that inspired and guided *this* stream of conscious manifestation.

lebeyt

If we know where we came from, we may better know where to go. If we know who we came from, we may better understand who we are! I wanna dedicate this work to my family the Tekele's.

bqz

Contents

iv

vi

Preface

Qal; ge'ez, ethiopic, ቃል : word

In the beginning was the word was it his or was it hers
Often times we contemplate duality
Ma'at: balance and chaos simultaneously
The universe coursing...the coldest heat
Storming electricity, Irony
Dangerous divinity moving towards ecstasy
Yang and yin
Sexual capacity
Puzzle piece attracting

...

Its seems every culture has their version
Here in lies mystic Abyssinian utterance in-person
The word in the beginning
With the gods and neverending

We send down rain from the sky with which we grow every type of noble species in pairs.

Luqman 31:10

The Path

Searching for the path like the son of man from Nazareth

like the order of the ancients, Melchzidek.

mystery system biz

like dorothy on her way to see the wiz

like dat lion lost his courage

Ma-tu-sala nine six nine on record

that's 8 threes 4 on each side
now what's better?
Henock escaping death. the fallen angels intent.
sacred geometrics. a lightning's decisive stretch.
a stars first breath. orgasmic love conquest. micro-cosmic
orbit. sexually healing all your organs.

Blessed. massaging what's tense.
freedom. dissolving stress. god's son manifest.
brazil. samba. black mamba. black excellence.
achievement. roc nation. sunday best. sacred texts.
Nubia. Kmt. Abyssinian genetics.
reaching for the highest cloud. movement. sound.
Muhammad. light project. on point. round.
expansive. divine timing. last second. down.
won the bet. H.I.M.
hard work n rest. creation manifest.
genet. Ghion.
the serpent. intellect.
what came next ...

Desert Omens

Will we go down in history fighting for our rights?

When will be the day that the fighting stops
when our lenses dilate at night?
no digits ticking time pretend.
sand hour watch. can't read a clock.

                      Nabta monolithic rock. desert omens.

can't count them numbers. but u wanna change the scene

controlled by a web of contortion.
the matrix, backward thinking...
Learn the fundamentals first, seek wisdom
like Solomon the mason
like the Ka-mite religion
like the Lasta lost kingdom

but them dark thoughts got me wilin
mad stylin
Black ninja
Sholin
Black magic
architectural semantics
defending righteous conscious status
the real Black Israelites. i'm Wu clanin.

Just This

J us heard justice ain't fair.

She sneaks out at night trying to find out what's out there.
And they say love is blind while they pushing plastic
Locked up in a vicious cycle of prison
stuck in time
trying to find a reason
         I'd rather put one up and enjoy the season
No finale for this Tru man show
off with their heads

Robin with an arrow

check out the signs

ain't got no pride to swallow

regurgitate. spit it back out. no need to follow.

      hard to picture your-self on a bakkle field with no amo

          watching the devils co-sign GMO

Hurts my soul to see a weak man on his knees

          begging for tomorrow

        Metamorphosis; let go of the fear n sorrow

         For the truth is never borrowed.

don't wanna be that naive girl

        looking for love at the dead of night

       not knowing it's gonna end up with a fight.

     choose thy Soul. ain't no return from this flight

          cabin pressure rise

        bout to switch off your light.

      watching it in slow-mo. think about your life

$\overline{\overline{\wedge}}$ Riddle of the Sphinx

Got me thinking like the book of thieves

You know I never stay I always leave.

Always thought that I was in the journey with my people

only to find out they all deceitful.

The author of my novel stay stoned like cobble

floating in space like the earth on its wobble.

Words flow through me when I switch to my channel

Aqueducts in my mind, the Red Sea canal.

Walking on water with words

confused by the lies I observe.

God Convo   ö

T he way I feel about you is beyond the feeling of a body.

For I God is the mother
You hold the holy grail or the chalice
My words may sound like a puzzle

gimmie more

More is given to you
How much u can basket and case makes u special

butterflies and etheric gases cycling through me
the dust of lost royalty

more like loyalty
coming clear after the dust
knowing self is a must
if pressure bus pipe
guess what it do to a human.
till u face your fears the ball is in your court

art versus my masculine muse reflection
but I'm an artist
my yin gives up my underlying obsession

u more like the art piece than the artist
for your thoughts are deep and complex
u know who tha artist is
the one that stays where the art is

ever seeking inspiration
paths to evolution defined
get high off conscious combinations
ancient symbolism refined

go on girl get on top
the way I like it Gill Scott!
everybody wanna rock the crown and it's a fact

final scene let the credits roll
hopein u find yo self in the midst of it all
when the needle skips and the song stops
no fat lady singing on the spot
dark goes my thoughts
searching for heaven
bn hell n back

Wise dome   ∞

Wish I had a penny for every-time niggas said I was

wise. Staring at the top of the pyramid searching for my
survival kit how imma survive…

Lyrical deity
let my words b the end of me
no formula for my thoughts

the plan is beyond infinity

        finding peace in creation ever-lasting

       searching for the story that never ends

          but flies passed me

lost understanding what's understood

while star gazing politicians scheme from the top

niggas fling hoop dream shots from the hood

how can I define struggle

when a child is born in a battle field

losing time when everything is hidden in plain sight

clear.

Can't blame a kid born in slavery coz all he know is bravery

world full of jealousy

        food chain designed strangely

            mortal kombat animality

for babylon shall fall

and my people stand tall

        standing tall from the east

         while the rest losing breath deceased.

dead man walking with-out the judge hitting tha gavel

XXX

no time for this man koz the crime don't fit
36 chamber grave pit
for love will take me where I belong to be
the Sun of man u can't take nothing from me.

Hail π

T he Sun of man

coming in cold in this damn land

searching the truth amongst convicted citizens

mans so wicked fighting for land watching the blood flow on

jerusalem sand

Looking for death while life looking at me strange

Fuck a rabbit hole. I seek change. Never beg

death is promised make my day.

xxxiii

bn dead since birth what u got to say

Black Thought •

F or justice let me down since birth

folded blind and gagged

    bn dragged thru the dirt

        no fear pon mi shirt

cautious walk. black fog. black thought.

black man. glass hour sand choose your life or slave the hand.

self captive. a captive land. captive tears on your mind.

Blurred sight.

        no army by ur side

    step light

more lies ahead   in plain sight …

Qal ÷ቀል

The king do what the king does without tha body I rise

struck a man's ego u get him for life
consciousness floating in a sea of vibration
searching for a complementary station to ride

what's found can't neva B searched
neva look for tha dark while its light
illuminate while u pass

> don't merge left keep right

∞

over stand all under-siege reflects what's inside
out of darkness creation spawned from the most-high

history is told by the war winners
hind sight gives u a bigger picture
dejavú is confirmation
fighting for rights should include spiritual violations
vampires vying for ur attention
sucking energy while parading as real friends

                              defecto de - mans
negating nature's essentials in her own image system
soul-less beings masquerading as suns of the sapien
            empty shells driven by drones of illusions
∞

the King do what he does to keep the peace
a united kingdom of Kings
No tolerance for euro-missionaries

                              to wash away sin
            Zemene Mesafint
            One aim
            One flag
            One enemy
                        One destination

Qaleesi ቀለሲ ((

Y ou serve me your words in sips

Tall glass with ice full to the brim
I drip anticipation while I wait on condensation.
Wondering when ur stratus clouds will float to my location

Drip drop goes the clock
Dark goes ur thoughts
Inside the atmospheric pressure
Feeding fire to icy rocks

I'm a sponge
Drinking up ur moisture like an oasis
Qal leading Qalisee to her new imperial stasis

The time between each thought is like a thousand miles of
                                                 sea
The way I thirst for all ur words keeps me faded
                                      like a fiend

Wet since the first text
High off ur frankincense
Drunk from ur intense
Tricked into submission

Saba, chambers of Solomon
More salty-sweet food offerings
Licking lips from salivation
Throat begging for lubrication
Thirsty for ur intuitions
While I wait and read and listen

Faucets steam n vapors rise activating all my chakras
I'm drinking all i can from u
                              U r my biblioteca
Ur words build my patience
                              le remerciement
Un-spoken conversations
Waking up with u alone

Depending on the next drop like it's my job to listen
I hang on every piece of thought like it's my only mission
I contemplate the cost forgetting lies and indecision
Never full of counting up ur drips of fire heated wisdom.

That Place

C an't wait to see it physically. For its everything I

wanted to see. Destiny manifest not manifested destiny.

Let ma words be alive
Can't let dis night get the best of mi
Playing chords of magic rushing towards ma everything
Take me to that place with no name where the silence
screams she wants more
well damn.

That place with no name is the place where I am
where I don't cling to mind states of oneness delusions

I go within.

Penetrating the blackness. Completion. Star movement.

Take me to that place where there was Word only
                              No division never lonely
                  Curving back towards the oneness of me
Sound, light and vibration
                    dance slowly.
Energy mathematics, emotion
                        Solarly

Back Thought   ~;)

Losing concentration when I look in your eyes, tryna

control this energy bubbling inside. One hundred thousand
thoughts per second got me tryna keep up. Your energetic
presence, got me straight heated. Fuck

While tryna keep up with my usual thought stream
I lift my eyes and see my Prince focusing

What was the point? I forgot. In my thoughts I am lost.
You are the Boss. Tell me ur wants and the cost.
                        Wisdom in your locks
             This conversing walk
Will all of this fade when our bodies sync up?
∞
Butterflies and etheric gases cycling through me

The dust of lost royalty
the gap widens
Admiring your height and complexion
DNA contemplations
The bones in your cheeks
to my real damn intentions

Rapid fire off top
Would u do it rough or more soft?
Would u pick me up...No. can I feel ur heart. Could u link
me up to a stream of your thoughts?

You only live once.
Your silence burns and I froze
Tryna keep my legs closed
my conversation slows
Rising serpent
keep low

Your intelligence got me focused inwardly
This heating resurgence got me backward thinking
Question, did I conjure u when I was dreaming?
All this time had my mind been receiving?
Perfection in the universal Law of Attraction
Realizing I can actually manifest my high version Black Man.

xlix

Corona ±✞

Disney fairytales in real life

      No white horse and carriage lift

                  Wordsmith

We moved beyond mis-concept.

           Energy bliss

Do u need me

Or are you the Universe's gift

Oceans of space and time up In the smoke drift

An elevation

Post imperial destabilization
Unspoken conversations
Family arrangements for expansion

I remember U in ur city
we met a few occasions
My root n solar plexus pulsing up the longing station
Ancestors speaking up for Un-attain-able relations

We must have been together in a long and deep dimension
Or could it be I'm mixing u with my daydream-versations?

Generational monarch
                    Abundant
Seeking shelter from a wild-west acquisition
                    Ironic
Ur Noble looks n phonics so appealing
                    mad exotic

Far from the Nile's meridian, the pyramid land.
                    Orien
Zion mountains
Turning tables since 73
No more kingdoms no more divine royalty

U want ur gold head west
blood diamonds MIA , NYC, Jacobs
But lineage knows no bounds
Duke and duchess lost and found
Floating in the clouds
Above mounds. Looking down. Feeling sound
Silent speech

A historical modern theme
To rise to the throne one needs a queen
   Empress Z 1916
   1930 Garvey's prophecy

Modern interpretations we both know
Historical reference, perfect genetic combo
Procreation
New kingdoms
Prestó
Envisage mi manifesto
   The life we could lead
   Inspiration daily
   Conscious considerating
   Mating recipes youth inseminating
   Debating mental stimulating
To Africa and back

No hesitation

My best life orchestrations.

Ur biggest fan consumed with life plans.

Castle comfort expenses creative freedom.

Empress vibes. A kept woman

One year ahead.

Do I wait it out or am I being led

Cash for love instead

what's my desire ... how will it end?

Makeda Menelik Solomon

Appreciate his presence

Keeps me hungry and yet still fed

He keeps me diving deep

Thirsty

Hanging on each word

like it's my life dependency

The globe and beyond

Any setting. Soul wedding

21st century

Zion coronation

Blessing

cn U hr mi nw ら

E‌motions of a child so frail

like laughing at chem trails
like a dog chasing its tail
Let your ego unveil knowledge of self prevail

Let love guide mi to my destiny
                              stop dreaming
fear is an illusion and innocence fleeting

capitalism posing as the greatest achievement
line up my gs
get online for your feeding
the web captures souls in a trap of 5 G tings
promoting caveman and roman livity
the intra-net broke what it mean to be free
programming distracting internal god speech

lvi

deluding with a clear connection
offering spiritual poverty recycling centers
knowledge of self is found in the deepest remembrance
in the folds of your sheets
in our electric connections

the DNA of ur blackness is magnetism in motion
n your hypnotic vibration can make earth leak new oceans.

Día de Muertos 0≠

Jacob's ladder climbing this life.

Skyscrapers and concrete jungle
        Forever I stand tall and humble
A vegan lion
contradiction never stumble.
Peace equals the outcome of the struggle
Shit might hurt like a kid watching his sand castle crumble

How can one be found when we ain't never lost?
They got us believing in ghosts. Black Renaissance.
Not the ones that rocked the fez and kept my people slave.
A generation of children growing up believing they dead

Sun of Yak   ↙⸱≐ʌ

Spit my truth.

My loved ones sold me en route. Bondage was never my
truth riding waves as sufferers do.
For a brief moment I am vulnerable on the search for what
I'm due.
Far from the lies of self

just beyond the borders of perfect chakric health

Truth seeking thru one's own lenses

Dissolving contorted pretenses

Chanting psalmic inclinations of the wise.

How deep I dive

For history been altered for a long time

And my thoughts designed
Eyes wide open and yet still blind
Realize the falsity within vanity and the sin. One's own mind
Liberation of thought the name of the game time

Lesson360   0

For history been altered n my thoughts designed

Eyes wide open but still blind

Realize the real lies within. Vanity n sin of one's mind

        Liberation of thought...the name of the game time

Discretion of the content that I let in. small circle of friends

The ability to see thru the darkness

Not getting uncomfortable when my thoughts spin

        looking between mind congestion

step away from grim judgment and scarcity thinking

A breathing manifestation of who I've always been

DNA connecting thousands of generations

        Life scars are my lessons.

           Make me genuine.

Sincerity. Universal existence.

Divine obelisk. Mystery system.

Prince. Pupil. High priest. Graduation

MeMuMi ᏃᎹ ᏃᎹ·ᎹᏆ.

T he body do what the body does.

Tuning us up

Never physical but tuned too u.

A guitar string touch

My perfect picture is not bn in you.

It comes from above

Maybe it's the idea of yo existence.

Invading subconscious

Each note I memorize n try to replay

You had the flute n keys & I had the bass

Alone I can't seem to make the rhythm fade

When we together it's about

                    where our fingers   place

Hearts pumping mellow

                    beats like   Dre

Blood rushing mimic dripping

                                        rain

Eyes singin sweet like Sade

Mind writing words yet un-sang

∞

Harmonics. Balance. Anthropic-trance

Dance

Space collapse

Time intersects. Blast off. Heat connect

                    Am i Trippin? Maestro or Magician?

                    Magic woman

Goddess

Spirit-walkin

Ancestren

Ark angelic descendant

uncovering my addictions.

I get caught up when I listen.

Music hits I feel no painin

Can do any thangs what I'm sayin

Escape all my limitations. Make mountains stand up on land

Sun. Dive deep blue oceans. Orbit Japanese space stations

∞

Shine bright. Tap in. Charge. Reset. Renew

Climax. Descend. Review. Round 2

∞

Harmonics of sound

I'm going down

Tryna resist

Pressed

Obsessed

Blessed

Maintaining interest

Intrigued

Waiting fo the next

Confident

Firm

Strong

Lean

Lyrics mean

Wet

Steam

Clean

Divine origins

Me Mu Mi

Ma ෴ ⁝

Sitting back reminiscing bout your existence got me

trippin.

Seems to me you the ultimate I seek in a woman

Ma and mi got wi floating

beyond feelings like we dopin

Make me think

how it'd be

if we made it to what we hopin

∞

watchin your body But it ain't the only I see

Heard your soul, touched yo truth- oceans of miles

ten shi

∞

I feel you as a whole, peeked into your soul
felt you more than I ever thought I wd kno

You the image of a true Nubian queen
never sexual
Felt your inside
without ever entering the physical
Intimacy-intellectual
Into-me-see
Intro-spec-tical

Enochisms. DNA. Complementary genetical
Qdus Mikael dimensional. Solar angels geometrical
The accounting of our current magnet historical processional

Steam

Hotter than July gimmicks or disguise

Whoever knew my thoughts could make ma *qal* revenu-ize

I gave free what's worth the heights

Too high to look down in they eye

Now I kno each word I spend

compounds in value

and in price

∞

Its so hot so I stay steaming

Dripping drops of subtle healing

Make unbelievers start believing

lxxv

My intuition-take the leading

Mystical insulation

Non-tactile thought relations

Holding close to incantations

Dreaming of no more separation

Longing for flesh interpretations

Universal confirmations

Freedom from heart n mind restrictions

One aim- one love- one destination

Excuses ع

Ever seeking inspiration

Paths to evolution defined
Get high off conscious combinations
Ancient Symbolism refined
On a never ending search for my ultimate Divine
Hoping that it will finally bring me all of that i left behind

But I'm an artist i need a muse
Between far and beneath few
But I'm an artist gleefully tortured by confuse
But I'm an artist painting landscapes of red right through my
blues. Is Linking heavens up with the dew
Led by the magnet that is you

lxxviii

Through waves of dimension portals too

My intention peeking tru

Art vs. my masculine muse reflection

But I'm an artist my yin gives up my underlying obsession

Pleasure pointing GPS on Igniting element connections

                                           Introspection

Artist excuses just to keep them sane men

X marks the spot in the midst of the chaos

Searching for the burning bush in the dark
Not an old man on his death bed trying to share a thought
For the great words are parables and allegory
following a man   and the lead
                              a component in chemistry
empty shell of a man tryna overcome the biology
not knowing the dirt is the true anatomy

The journey is the check of self

finding out one's worth.

        forget the scale.

Justice ain't blind

she sneak peaking in the darkest night

never catch me complaining about what's right

never been mesmerized by the glitch and the lights

Primordial man

blessed with ancient sights.

        Jacob's ladder climbing this life

Skyscrapers and concrete jungle

Forever I stand tall and humble

A vegan lion contradiction never stumble.

Peace the outcome of the struggle

Shit might hurt like a kid watching his sand castle crumble.

How can one be found when we ain't never lost?

        They got us believing in ghosts.

Inspiration coming short like a mirage

Suns of the golden age trying to capture some land

With the illusion of freedom at hand

Plymouth rock ∂¶

I should B hold accountable

For holding the seeds of deception
Watching d'evils roam free with no precaution
Now we stuck on Plymouth rock with no probation
Tobacco plants and mine fields
Old stories of us running wild
No shackles but still trapped wishing for the days I was
strapped

With the iron I graze the land
For this seed will grow on concrete
Like the innocent blood that they shade on thee streets

There is no king and I

        But I & I. James Cagney

        Let the pigs bleed pon thee alley.

        Fuck your humanity

Tackling hunger with a telephone cable

Chasing happiness ✕

I'll be happy tomorrow

Tomorrow never comes

Chasing time that's borrowed

Chasing happiness forever

I'll be happy tomorrow

Is a vicious cycle

lxxxvii

And a tantalizing sorrow

Remaining at a relatively even state of desire

Running while your feet is on fire

The rat race to happiness is today's old new

Old replaces new

Glamorize tomorrow while u getting used

When we glamorize the future we glamorize the negatives

Love in the present is catch 22

Live in the present

Look beyond the initial glow

Of a thing not the glamour of thinking of tomorrow

Stop chasing rainbows

The more things change the more the same goes

Concentrate on happiness today

And guarantee that joy follows

Lucy

Ma true image of female u are!

Never sexual

will never lead u on.

but u exceptional

Felt yo inside. No recreational...

Top shelf. Thorough bred. Right angles all symmetrical.

The core of nature's over flow. Crystalline. In-tro-spec-tical

Activated chakras and sol.

Greens plus h2o.

What they think vs. what u know

in truth

Mustard seed faith

swell into sweet fruit

rays n vibrations drumming down her deep roots

Ma lucy's Afar-ness give birth to my youth

Poetic Justice ° 𐤉𐤃

What's the word that's never been said?

The thought that's never been described
It's all been said and done under the sun.
Like a fatherless child.

Who's gonna son I and I?
Whose gonna ride?
It's a matter of flow. Least resistance. Following the vibe

Poetic justice.
Where else can one ponder celestial greatness?
Matter.
Passion. Platonic solids. Sacred
Fire burning cores n igniting action
foreign language defining spiritual abstraction.
Biological attraction.
Science mapping.

Thoughts dancing
Mental integration over miles of sea.
Where I wanna be.
repatriate or retreat.
Locked in a cave focused on dream state reality
watching shadows on the wall...

Desire

What's the point of desire?

Keeping my core on fire
my mind wired
how many ways can I say inspired?
Infatuated. Intangibly related.
Heart bumping word, sound and power vibrations

To think all these years were preparation
What is this elation?
How can a Magnet experience intimidation
swimming in a sea of separation
On the way westing
Fuck waitin

Mind anticipations imagination or reality
Dreams on a movie screen
Executive direction ... on the spot
writing in new love scenes
Run it back
Climax
Fade to black

Frequency relay
Happiness delay
Gods molded clay

Masculine perfection
Divine inception. Symmetry.
Mind-set, aura, sound.
Width, length, shade. 80% cacao
Bitter sweet. Highland origins in the clouds
Heavenly
Clean
Ready to return to mi. Like the Sah-bah. Abyssinian Hajj.
Deep
Diabolically down.
Space and time. 10 g's
2020
Two dimes
One dub
Double up
When we merge we are one
that mean desire
neverending
like the Sun

Ra ⊙ ራስ

I want to bask in your shine

I want u to light mi up
        and give me tan lines
I want u to charge me with your heat
I want to study ur luminosity in peace

I want you to crown mi in the night
I want your magnet pulling towards my Nile

I want to bathe in your glory
I want to watch you rise in the morning

I wanna watch u sinking in the west
        Your face speaks hidden wisdom of the ancients

I want you to toast mi goldn brown
I want to see your shadow on the ground
I want you to seep into my lenses
I want to dissolve all pretenses
        I want you to see me to through your Solstices

I want you to lead mi thru both your equinoxes
        I want you to soothe mi with your spinning
I want to time my eclipse and our conjuncting
I
want
you
to
sprinkle
sparkle
seeding…

And I saw heaven opened and behold a white horse; and he that
sat upon him was called faithful and true and in righteousness he
doth make war. His eyes were as flames of fire and on his head he
wore many crowns; and he had a name written that no man
knew, but he himself… and his name is called the WORD…

Rev 9:11

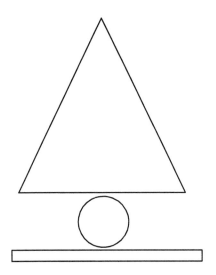

CPSIA information can be obtained
at www.ICGtesting.com
Printed in the USA
BVHW052329041021
618136BV00011B/314

9 781732 087527